Dear Parents and Educators,

W9-BTI-030

Welcome to Penguin Young Readers! As parents and educators, you know that each child develops at his or her own pace—in terms of speech, critical thinking, and, of course, reading. Penguin Young Readers recognizes this fact. As a result, each Penguin Young Readers book is assigned a traditional easy-to-read level (1–4) as well as a Guided Reading Level (A–P). Both of these systems will help you choose the right book for your child. Please refer to the back of each book for specific leveling information. Penguin Young Readers features esteemed authors and illustrators, stories about favorite characters, fascinating nonfiction, and more!

Lion, Tiger, and Bear

LEVEL **4**

GUIDED READING LEVEL **N**

This book is perfect for a **Fluent Reader** who:
• can read the text quickly with minimal effort;
• has good comprehension skills;
• can self-correct (can recognize when something doesn't sound right); and
• can read aloud smoothly and with expression.

Here are some **activities** you can do during and after reading this book:
• Discuss: It is amazing that an American black bear, a Bengal tiger, and an African lion are such good friends. Discuss the differences between the three animals and how going through a difficult time together allowed them to overcome their differences and be friends.
• Fiction vs. Nonfiction: Fiction stories include events that are made up. Nonfiction stories deal with facts and events that are real. This is a nonfiction book. Discuss the elements of nonfiction and make a list of facts that you learned about Leo, Baloo, and Shere Khan.

Remember, sharing the love of reading with a child is the best gift you can give!

—Bonnie Bader, EdM
    Penguin Young Readers program

*Penguin Young Readers are leveled by independent reviewers applying the standards developed by Irene Fountas and Gay Su Pinnell in *Matching Books to Readers: Using Leveled Books in Guided Reading*, Heinemann, 1999.

For my best friend, Tom,
who also likes BLTs—KR

PENGUIN YOUNG READERS
Published by the Penguin Group
Penguin Group (USA) LLC, 375 Hudson Street, New York, New York 10014, USA

USA | Canada | UK | Ireland | Australia | New Zealand | India | South Africa | China

penguin.com
A Penguin Random House Company

Penguin supports copyright. Copyright fuels creativity, encourages diverse voices,
promotes free speech, and creates a vibrant culture. Thank you for buying an authorized edition
of this book and for complying with copyright laws by not reproducing, scanning, or distributing any
part of it in any form without permission. You are supporting writers and allowing Penguin to
continue to publish books for every reader.

The publisher does not have any control over and does not assume any
responsibility for author or third-party websites or their content.

Photo credits: cover, pages 3, 10–17, 19–48: © Noah's Ark Animal Rehabilitation Center, Inc.;
pages 4–5: © Thinkstock, photo by agafapaperiapunta; page 6: © Thinkstock, photo by ewastudio;
page 7: © Thinkstock, photo by Lynn_Bystrom; pages 8–9, 46: (map) © Thinkstock, image by rtguest;
page 8: (bear) © Thinkstock, image by Lynn_Bystrom; page 9: (lion) © Thinkstock, image by Eric
Isselée; page 9: (tiger) © Thinkstock, image by Eric Isselée; page 18: © Thinkstock, photo by Amawasri.

You can find out more about Noah's Ark Animal Sanctuary at www.noahs-ark.org.

Text copyright © 2015 by Kate Hurley. All rights reserved. Published by Penguin Young Readers,
an imprint of Penguin Group (USA) LLC, 345 Hudson Street, New York, New York 10014.
Manufactured in China.

Library of Congress Cataloging-in-Publication Data is available.

ISBN 978-0-448-48336-8 (pbk)   10 9 8 7 6 5 4
ISBN 978-0-448-48337-5 (hc)   10 9 8 7 6 5 4 3 2 1

Lion, Tiger, and Bear

by Kate Ritchey
with photographs from Noah's Ark Animal Sanctuary

Penguin Young Readers
An Imprint of Penguin Group (USA) LLC

In Africa's grasslands, lions hunt in packs.

In the jungles of Asia, Bengal tigers compete with other carnivores for food.

In North American forests, American black bears live alone and forage for nuts, berries, and small animals to eat.

These three wild animals normally would never meet—but what would happen if they did?

One morning in the summer of 2001,
the police in Atlanta, Georgia, were
searching a basement. All of a sudden,
one of the policemen heard something.
Was someone hiding there?

No!

Much to his surprise, he had heard a baby African lion, a baby Bengal tiger, and a baby American black bear! What were they doing there?

The person who lived in the house was keeping these animals as pets, but he wasn't taking very good care of them. The cubs were hurt and unhealthy.

The police removed the three-month-old cubs from the home. But what now? Who would take care of them?

Noah's Ark Animal Sanctuary heard about the animals. Noah's Ark, which is not far from Atlanta, takes care of many abused and unwanted animals, such as monkeys, wolves, peacocks, parrots, and horses.

The caretakers at Noah's Ark offered to take in the hurt cubs. They even gave the cubs names: Leo the lion, Shere Khan the tiger, and Baloo the bear, calling them "BLT" (for *bear, lion,* and *tiger*) for short!

When the cubs arrived at Noah's Ark, they were still very sick and hurt. Right away, they went to an animal doctor, called a veterinarian (say: vet-er-uh-NAIR-ee-uhn).

Shere Khan had not been eating the right kind of food.

Leo had been kept in such a tiny cage that the skin on his nose had been rubbed off.

Baloo was in the worst shape of the three. He had been wearing a harness that was too small, which was digging into his skin. It was very painful, and he needed surgery to have it removed.

When Baloo was taken away for his surgery, Leo and Shere Khan became upset. They cried and looked for him. They even refused to eat.

What was going on? The caretakers were puzzled.

Here were three animals from three different continents, who would not have been friends out in the wild. But now they cared for one another. What an unlikely group of friends!

As soon as Baloo returned from surgery, Leo's and Shere Khan's behavior was back to normal. What now?

The caretakers had been planning to keep the animals in different areas of Noah's Ark, yet now they knew that they couldn't do that. The cubs had survived a frightening time together, and as a result, had become like brothers. The caretakers couldn't possibly separate this new family!

The people at Noah's Ark raised the three cubs together. They fed them with baby bottles until they were old enough for real food.

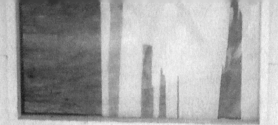

The Noah's Ark staff watched BLT closely for several years to make sure the animals didn't start fighting as they got older.

But Leo, Shere Khan, and Baloo remained close.

As BLT grew up, they got *big*! They
needed a home that was big, too, so their
friends at Noah's Ark built a special
space just for them. Their home is an
open lawn with a creek running through
the grass, because Baloo and Shere Khan

like being in the water. It also has
a one-room house with a big porch
where the animals can sleep and relax.
Although the place is surrounded by a
fence, the animals still have plenty of
room to play.

Baloo is a gentle bear, but he also likes to be in charge. The big bear weighs over 800 pounds! He likes to eat fruits, vegetables, nuts, and meat—and he really loves sweets. Oreos and Tootsie Pops are Baloo's favorite treats.

Leo is very quiet and calm, and he sleeps a lot. He can be a little grumpy, too! He roars when Shere Khan pounces on him too many times. Sometimes Leo likes to pretend he is the boss, but he knows Baloo actually is. Leo weighs 430 pounds. Since lions are carnivores, Leo eats mostly meat. But he also eats a special food for wild big cats.

Shere Khan is the most playful of the friends, and he is always pouncing on Baloo and Leo. Sometimes he likes to cause trouble.

One of his favorite tricks is biting
his friends on their backsides and then
running away! He weighs 360 pounds.
Like Leo, he eats meat and the special
cat food.

Leo, Shere Khan, and Baloo eat, sleep, and play together. They wrestle with one another, and they share toys like balls, a tire swing, and cardboard animals.

They show their love by licking one another and rubbing heads. Shere Khan looks like a house cat when he rubs heads with Baloo!

Just like human friends, sometimes BLT become frustrated with one another. Baloo even bites Leo on the eyebrow when he is upset with him! (Not hard enough to hurt him, though.)

All three will slap the others with their paws, and they will sleep far away from one another if they're angry. But in the end, they always forgive their friends.

Sometimes unlikely friends turn out to be the best ones! Just look at BLT: No one would have guessed that an African lion, a Bengal tiger, and an American black bear could get along, but they do!

If you want to see BLT in person, you can visit them at Noah's Ark Animal Sanctuary in Locust Grove, Georgia. The sanctuary cares for over 1,000 animals in addition to Leo, Shere Khan, and Baloo!